Sad Bitch Poetry

Ember Gray

Published by Ember Gray, 2022.

While every precaution has been taken in the preparation of this book, the publisher assumes no responsibility for errors or omissions, or for damages resulting from the use of the information contained herein.

SAD BITCH POETRY

First edition. October 15, 2022.

ISBN: 979-8215849460

Written by Ember Gray.

Also by Ember Gray

Watch This Possum Blossom
Sad Bitch Poetry

Table of Contents

want 1

koi no yokan...........2

cliff's edge 3

What happened to the sun...........7

good luck 8

built...........9

Vegas can wait 10

Kalopsia 11

promise me [nothing]........... 13

walk 15

hush........... 16

seeking: peace of mind........... 17

spilt milk........... 18

for you 19

handling it 21

cutting room floor........... 22

connection/abandon........... 27

hourglass 28

fallen phoenix 31

gone........... 33

The nymph and the lumberjack 34

piano in the rain 35

Favorite........... 37

stitched........... 38

on my deathbed........... 40

haunted 41

October 15........... 43

988 44

One step...........46

epitaph 50

pray 52

letter 54

hope 60

for my friends and family who consistently support me.

for my dogs who put up with my crying.

Consume me
I want to drown in your love
and feel your passion
fill me to the brim
as it spills into our life.
Burn my lips
with such ferocious kisses
I'm ravenous for your touch.
I crave you in every
possible way.

The moment I saw you,
I knew I would fall in love.
I spent weeks, months
trying to wait for you.

I needed you in my life,
to be my life.
My future was now
going to be with you.

I gave you every inch,
every ounce,
every part of me
my love was only for you.

I was there through your worst.
I was there for the best.
I was there for you.
I was there.
I was.

I wrap my silver cardigan tightly
against my pale lace nightgown
as I amble out the door.
Somewhere nearby thunder rumbles slowly,
threatening to release its fury upon the land.
I welcome it.
I haven't felt understood
about the storm that rages within me for so long.
The dark gray sky stirs the heavy clouds,
whisking them together into a beautiful painting
a few shades darker than my cardigan.
Should the rain decide to fall though,
it will match in color.
The chains of the swing you built for us
rattle at the edge of the porch.
The grass beneath my bare feet
is soft as I walk to the cliff's ledge.

Looking over the edge, I keep a slight distance.
I know the grass becomes slick
and can pull unsuspecting beings down
its long rocky side and into the turbulent waters below.
Sometimes I imagine myself taking a couple steps closer.
Sometimes I wonder if I shouldn't be led to the icy waters
that took you away from me.
I peer into the navy veil
as the waves bring sparkling crests to the surface.

EMBER GRAY

Anger and sadness churn within my chest
as it churns in the sea.
Grief and isolation swirl with betrayal behind my ribs,
the cage trying to keep them deep inside.
I'm so tired of keeping it all inside though.
I yearn to release my anguish as the clouds do.

I sit on the damp earth and take it all in,
my fingers digging into the dewy soil.
I clench my hands tight and rip out whatever flora I touch.
Emerald blades of grass scatter my gown
as I open my palm to let them fall.
Dusky mud stains my cardigan.
The wind sends wisps of my long hair behind me,
the sea mist glistening on my face.
The cool salty water blankets my cheeks
and conceals the salty tears that escape my eyes.
Only out here do I dare let them out.
I can pretend it's the mist stinging them.
I refuse to be perceived as weak,
but I am so alone in this quiet solitude.

Thunderous grumbles have grown louder
as the sky takes on a darker hue now nearly charcoal.
Plump drops begin to fall
and it takes only minutes for the rain to soak my bones.
Shivers envelop my skin as I stare into the endless gloomy sky.
I want to stand and run to the house,
to seek shelter from the weather
as it thrashes trees and spills down from tragic clouds.

SAD BITCH POETRY

Instead, I make my way to the cliff's edge again,
this time getting mere inches
from the rim that holds me 200 feet above the water.
I gaze disheartened at the murky waves
as they torment me with the memory of losing you.
Dejected waves crash roughly into the rocky side.
Desire to be at the bottom pulls at me
from somewhere within my body.
A ghastly vision of the cliffs I stand on
cascading to the water,
cut deep by the relentless attacks
of the wave etched notches,
fills my head.
Perhaps if my end comes due to an unfortunate accident,
I won't feel guilty.
I shake my head vehemently.

You were my paramour.
You still are.
I will never let you be forgotten.
If I must remain on this cursed cliff,
I shall bury my roots deep beneath the ground.
You will never be alone below the water's crest,
for my sorrow of missing you
keeps me tethered to this damned ledge.
Perhaps one day I will let the cliff take me as it took you,
so we might be reunited
after such a meaningless and wretched life without you.

EMBER GRAY

anger

Last night
the sun didn't set.
It fell.

The sky caught fire
blanketing the world
with ash and soot.

The bright orange sphere
paled in comparison
to the rage she emanated.

Auburn streaks doused
her golden hair as charcoal dust
smeared her cheeks.

Blood, sweat, and tears
she would have given you the sky.
Now, there is nothing.

She stands tall
rage radiating,
it will only be warmer tomorrow.

No one could ever love you
the way that I do.
No one could understand
the way your mind works like I do.
No one could have the patience.
No one would put up with your torment.
Have fun fucking over the next one.

Time goes fast
and slow.
I sleep when I should be awake
while the night torments me
with such vivid memories of you.

Can you still feel me
under your fingertips?
Do you think of me
when you touch your hair?
Have you missed my embrace
when you needed to cry?

I was built to love you,
only you.

Another trip planned.
Another trip abandoned.

"It would've been a lot of fun"
Was all you could muster.

This was supposed to be a celebration.
My 28th in Vegas with the one I love.
Commemorating a dream fulfilled.
Visiting a new part of us.

I guess Vegas can wait.

Kalopsia

How dare you tell me that it wasn't real.
Prove to me that you didn't mean it.

I don't believe you
there's no way
it wasn't wholly
phantasmagorical.
The late nights talks,
countless I love yous,
starry nights,
flowers.

The sparkle in your eye
the softness in your voice
your skin against mine
as you held me close

It wasn't just excitement.
I loved you hard
and you loved me.

Remember when you said
you couldn't live without me?

you're doing just fine,
but I'm wishing for my grave.

Everything we had
meant the world.

Hold me close
as you slit my throat.
Look me in the eyes
as you pour the salt.
Whisper you love me
as you scald my flesh.
Say my name
as you mangle my heart.

promise me nothing
as you annihilate me.

EMBER GRAY

bargaining

Barren streets lay out beneath me,
only falling leaves join
as the cold wind blows.

The silence hurts my ears
nearly as much
as your parting words.

Solid ground seems to be crumbling
as my timid steps
cause me to reconsider.

The lies you told
lie behind me
while I try not to look back.

What good is sorry
when our own world
is now in mayhem.

Save yourself and
take what you need,
don't worry about the fallout.

I saw a red door over the bridge.
A large ladder stood in front,
Bad luck should you want to enter.

I made my way through the water
Waist deep in my want,
Feeling myself halfway home.

A black cat crossed my path
As I climbed onto the bank,
Curiosity in its eyes.

Dripping with trepidation,
My steps were rushed
Reaching the gate quickly.

Inner voices began screaming,
"Don't bother knocking!"
Do they know something I don't?

Someone inside lit a candle
As I shiver in my frigid clothes.
I don't belong here.

Tell me to stay, please.
I'm begging
I can't go through this life alone.

Maybe I need you.
Remind me, I'm alive.

I can't tell if I'm here.
There's no way to know.
Will you wake me up?

The small glass
crashes to the floor.
I fall next to it
weeping as I pick up
the broken shards.
White liquid
soaks my socks.
Fierce tears
stain my cheeks.

It was never about
the milk.

I have unwritten letters
for you.
Things that have happened
and you were the first
person I wanted to tell.

I have an unsaved playlist
for you.
Songs that remind me
of you
and the music
you would like.

I have an imaginary list
for you.
Places and restaurants
that would fill
our days
with memories.

I have a hollow in my essence
for you.
carved for the body
and psyche
meant only
for my person.

EMBER GRAY

I have lost myself
without you.
Etched into every aspect
of my being
I will never be whole
with you missing.

I have my shattered heart
for you.
It's still
yours
should you ever
want it back.

I am and I am not.

The crying has stopped.
The anger has subsided.
I make it to work.

But I've crossed over.
A darker, more sinister place.
Nearly no feeling.

I want to quit.
I want to stop.
I can't do this.

I'm on the cutting room floor,
desperately grasping for any scraps
of a future I could salvage.
How often must I be back here?
Sprawled on the cold floor,
thousands of memories lay out beneath me.
Cutting together a new life,
while trying not to lament too long
over the one that is now destroyed.
I don't know how many more times
I can stitch myself back together.

Sifting through nearly two years
of my own history,
my eyes sting with hot tears.
Anger and regret and grief leak
as I wipe them away.
They feel similar to the crimson blood
that routinely drips from my wrists and thighs.
If I sat here naked,
everything would be tarnished with my agony.
So I bandage myself and wear long sleeves
to ensure a quick swipe
of my cheek will keep things dry.
I have to get this done.

Reels of us play across the room,

loving moments of affection and happiness.
The background noise of laughing,
heartfelt I love yous,
long talks about our dreams.
I tune them out.
They have no place in the new work.
I would almost prefer the deafening silence over this.
But I let it run.
Maybe it can distract me
as I rummage for anything worth saving.
I don't have the capacity
to focus on what I'm looking at,
what I need to let go.
If I do,
I'll be a puddle of despair
and nothing will be saved.
I sigh deeply
and look at the small frames in my hands.

And that's just it, isn't it?
Life isn't about grand, big gestures.
No, life is made up of small moments,
frames of love and joy and support.
Fragments of tiny efforts
that fills you with a sense of comfort.
I'm supposed to go through all of this,
frame by frame?
Then carefully make a new life for me?
Just me?
How am I supposed to sort through everything,

EMBER GRAY

when you play a part in all aspects of my day?
Any shoddy form of a new future
I haphazardly patch together
will still have you in it.
You've changed me and the way I think.
The way I feel.

Long strips of translucent film
slide through my hands quickly,
fresh blood prickling from new cuts.
The edges are smudged,
flecks of my current heartbroken self penetrating it.
My hands are both numb and tingling.
At this point, any wound is familiar.
I welcome the physical hurt
that thinks it can combat the torment boiling inside me.

I glance to the wall,
noticing one of the memories
seems to be playing in slow motion.
Maybe the projector has gotten too hot,
I've been letting it run for days now.
I stare at the scene,
not even recognizing the person shown.
I know it's me.
I mean,
why would someone else's memories
be playing in this dismal room?
But,
I don't recognize her.

SAD BITCH POETRY

She looks so...happy.
She has a dazzling brightness in her eyes
as she stands next to her paramour.
They are looking at the night sky
while he names the constellations.
She's barely even looking at the stars,
her eyes trained on him.
Soft tears brim her eyes
as she's enveloped in his arms.

I remember that night.
To this day, it may have been the happiest,
purest night I've ever experienced.
And now, that's all it will be.
A passing moment in a life that had to end.
I stumble to the back of the room
where a small mirror hangs crooked.
I gaze at my reflection.
I look deep into the mirror
but I don't see myself.
This woman is harsh, haggard.
Where the girl in the film had shining eyes
–full of life and love–
these eyes hold dying embers,
the light barely flickering.
By the look of her defeated and worn face,
only ashes will remain soon.
It doesn't look like she has much left in her.

Collapsing to the floor,

EMBER GRAY

the broken and damaged film
littered around me feels bleak and meaningless.
Why am I going through all of this?
The woman in the mirror has given up,
why should I continue?
Piecing together shreds
into a jagged, pathetic life,
what's the use?
The projector continues as I lay.
Happy sounds of our past
torments me as my light dies excruciatingly slowly.

I risked what I had
hungry for someone to know
someone accepting.

Throwing it all down
ready to fight til the end
ready to give all.

The risk was wasted
having tasted connection
now left abandoned.

Deserted and scared
I don't know what to do here
frantic thoughts buzzing.

Please, I needed you
I can't go through this alone
I'll lose to myself.

Darkness is growing
consuming me completely
where has the light gone?

Glass shatters all around me
my world crashing to the floor
as the sands of my hourglass
pour into a ruddy pile.

Empty shelves surrounding
as I struggle to grasp anything
falling, falling,
a gentle yearning pulls me faster.

There's a whistle somewhere
beyond this cramped room
it sounds like music
in the middle of such distress.

I beg for them to keep it down
I can't think as it grows louder.
Burying it below
keeping my attention on the shards.

Sprint to the sink
where the water is overflowing
spilling and flooding the floor
mixing with my ruined sand.

Trust has been broken

and it makes me cry
struggling to come up
with a new plan, a new beginning.

The complicated harmony
screeching from the other room
penetrates and assaults
my ears as it escalates.

Frantic glances around the room
lead me to spot a small bottle
discreetly hidden by my past self,
the label reads *do not drink*.

Jealously overtakes me
considering how content I used to be
as the glass bottle touches my lips
swallowing what tastes like Vanilla Coke.

EMBER GRAY

depression

fallen phoenix

Scorched,
my wings have been maimed.
Once strong and fierce,
large and intimidating,
now are irrevocably damaged.

Flaming,
my hearth is no longer mine.
A place of comfort and home,
warm and inviting,
now billows black smoke.

Fallen,
my body cannot support me.
My evaporating strength,
scant and depleting,
I simply fall away.

Look at my mutilated form
and say to hold out for hope.
My flaming hearth
could offer rebirth.

But a veil covers me
as black as the smoke
smothering my breath.
Exhausted, suffocating,

EMBER GRAY

I hide my tears
as I surrender.

32

The girl you knew is no longer here.
My body, a husk of who I was
taking away my identity.

The girl you loved is no longer here.
A bleeding heart has ruptured
taking away my warmth.

she's gone.
I'm gone.
gone.

I will never be her again.
Would you want me still?
My broken self,
a hardened shell
encasing dark chaos.

Once affectionate and bright
I now revel in the anguish.

forgotten and strangled
you would not recognize me.

The nymph and the lumberjack

A nymph roamed the forest
desperate to find a home.
One day she met a lone lumberjack
desperate for support.

She gave every ounce of herself
attempting to make the lumberjack
see the beauty in life.
She built a home in him
that sheltered and protected.

She should have known
a lumberjack will cut down
the very forest she stood for.

Leaving her alone
and broken,
the lumberjack moved on.

Another late night with no sleep.
I don't know if it's my mind relentlessly buzzing
or the thunderstorm growling beyond my windows,
but I have given up any chance to rest.
I reach for my coat and head out the door,
locking it behind me.

I don't know what brought me here.
The piano keys *plink* lightly
as fat raindrops pelt against the painted wood.
I want to sit at the bench,
place my finger where yours
have traced this damned instrument so many times.

How many minutes have I listened to you play?
The summer air,
warm and inviting
as your music drifts from your hands,
surrounding us.
The songs you've written,
the melodies you created as you played,
the tunes you learned from others.

So many bright and sunny mornings spent with you,
coffee in hand as we breathe in the fresh air.

Now I sit in the cold rain

EMBER GRAY

only clunky plucks to keep me company.
Heavy clouds raining down on me
Soaking me to the bone.
Shivers are relentless as I let myself cry.

I will never get to listen to your beautiful music again.
The piano is worthless.

Favorite

I can't go to any of my favorite places
Without reminders of you.
Everywhere we went
Became my new favorite.

Craft stores and farmers markets
Coffee shops and comedy clubs
Book stores and restaurants
Theaters and arcades
Gardens and pianos
Festivals and fairs

Maybe it's because
You were my favorite.

Reaching for my thread
I begin to sew myself
together again.

How many more times
must I stitch broken pieces
while my heart comes loose?

Sharp, tiny needles
piercing my flesh that's bleeding
a familiar pain.

Burning with metal,
the only way of feeling
simulated joy.

Stuck between too much
and not feeling it at all,
an exhausting line.

I drag my frown up
forcing a smile that's doctored
crimson streams my throat.

Manipulated,
A dark smokescreen concealing

my mutilation.

Stitched into my chest
sutured with shaking fingers
"Stay Strong". "You Are Loved".

Everyone talking
too many people at once
it doesn't change things.

With these reminders
now etched into my being
will the voices stop?

Pretty chains bind me to my bed,
sparkling faintly with what little light
sneaks into the room.

Bandages hug my wrists
even though I want the cuffs
slicing my flesh.

Fresh wounds appear daily,
even if I spend my time asleep
brief tranquility from my mind.

Heavy cries and wine elixir
mixing with my sleeping pills
diminishing my waking day.

No one is coming to visit
as my memories fade,
the clocks have stopped.

do you feel my ghost,
or has the memory of us
began to evanesce?

the empty space
washed in your bed,
can you still smell my scent?

hollow and stripped
drifting between worlds
I yearn for any form
of resolution.

aimless and airy,
these quiet rooms
my own haunted home.

no lights within my halls,
my candles haven't burned
since you hold the match.

overgrown is my garden
as weeds choke my roots,
overtaking the flowers.

dusty drapes hang

EMBER GRAY

layers of filth against the panes,
cracked and forgotten
I don't know when I last felt the sun.

shivering without bones
holding nothing but pain,
my chest heaves.

a desolate cavern
fractured beyond repair,
worthless.

I revel in the shadows
as they allow me
the space to weep.

my birth
my death

I don't want those who may
mourn me
to have sorrow year round.

So I'll end my life
the day I arrived.

One date to remember.

Last night was a very bad night.
I called the Crisis Hotline
and spoke to a woman,
telling her I didn't know
if I should go to the hospital.

I was scared
I was going to do
something permanent.

She helped talk things out with me
and suggested a few ways to calm down.
By the time we were done
I did feel better,
but I've truly never been that close to suicide.
I was seriously ready
to get in my car and check myself in.
The woman on the Crisis Hotline
told me that the hospital is last resort,
but if I feel that I should go, to go.

I've been having a lot of really bad days like that,
so I need to get something fixed.

I've contacted
my therapist and psychiatrist
this morning to get appointments set up.

SAD BITCH POETRY

I'm not doing well at all
and it's getting to a scary point
where I don't know how to stop it.
45

Just wanted to let you know.

On the ledge of a bridge,
blood dripping from my wrists
into the cold dark water thrashing below.
Not even the moon wants to show on this night.
The sky is black with dimly speckled stars
behind heavy gray clouds blotting them out.

The water and sky
seem to have no separation
as I look toward what I imagine is the horizon.
Heavy clouds threaten to release their own storm,
but so far it's just been for show.
I've stood here nearly 20 minutes,
wishing for a gust of angry wind
to blow me right over the edge.
My woes and sorrow wash away
as my body drifts to the bottom of the sandy grave.

But no wind has taken action for me.
It will be up to me if I take a step.
As seconds pass,
that first step,
my last,
feels more welcoming.

The longer I stand, the more I want to fall.
Head first.

SAD BITCH POETRY

I go into everything head first, no hesitation.
It should be correct to end my life
the same way I lived it.
Perhaps that's what brought me here.

Putting my entire being into love,
risking all for a taste of the home I've never had.
A security and comfort that is forever just out of reach.
I can see it,
I can smell it,
I can almost touch it.

But I will never have it.
The loving home of another,
apparently not meant for me.
It's so cruel, life teases me with it.

Just one step.

One small step,
and I can be free.
Free from the turmoil of my bones and mind.
Making stupid decisions
in a foolish attempt to live a life worth keeping.
To find any reason to hang on a little longer.
Desperately,
on a never ending search for a will to live.
I'm tired.
I'm exhausted.

EMBER GRAY

I've done everything I can think of,
vain attempts to quench this thirst of meaning.
Yet,
I will never find it.
I will forever have a deep chasm within me,
a black hole only growing bigger with time.
I'm beyond repair.

How nice it would be to finally rest.
To finally feel nothing,
a welcomed change
from the constant barrage
of complicated thoughts and emotions
that requires too much attention.
Constant noise and static filling me,
seeping into my life.
Oh, how content would that make me.
Such quiet
after a life of incessant crowding of my mind.
The voices and memories bent on my destruction.

Maybe they should win.
My only form of solace,
knowing they won't leave me alone.
While I stare into the emptiness,
my fears and agitations are always right there.
Turbulence churning within my chest,
trying to break my rib cage and reach the water.

SAD BITCH POETRY

Breathe deep.
The scent of the river penetrates my nostrils
as the cool air touches my bare skin.
Hairs stand on end,
as if they too yearn for the depths beneath.
Pulling me toward it,
making me anxious to leap.
Not just step,
but jump.
Freefall into eternity.
I want to.
I want to let go
and let death caress my broken body
as I vanish from this world.

Let me feel nothing.
Let me finally be free.
My feet hit the air as I close my eyes.

Silver moonlight illuminates
a familiar name upon the tombstone.
My mistakes and regrets
catch up to me as I sit beside it.

Dearly departed rest,
at least that's what I thought.
Now it feels as if this graveyard
is home to my captured soul.

I'm losing touch with this world
reaching out for the decor,
flowers and ribbons
from those who loved me.

Not fully human
though, not yet a ghost.
Stuck between realms
almost worse than before.

Staring at the trees nearby
a few birds nest in sparse branches.
The hardest part is not being able
to explain why I had to leave.

SAD BITCH POETRY

[not yet] acceptance

51

I gather my courage
and step into the old church.
White lace lines the aisle
as I stumble forward.

I sit in the front pew
completely alone.
Tilting my head
I hold my hands.

It's all so unfamiliar,
I feel like a fraud.
But I have
nowhere else
to go.

I pray.
The words are fast and strange on my tongue.
I pray.
Begging for my last second chance.
I pray.
My eyes are misty and the cross is out of focus.

Would God even consider me?
A rough swallow of sorrow goes down.
My hands a shaking,
clammy near the cold altar.

SAD BITCH POETRY

Sanctuary in more ways than one,
Yet I still don't feel welcomed.
Pretty words adorn the lavish walls
Stained glass bleeding red onto me.

Rituals deeply rooted
yet not in my soul
I pray.

It's all I have left.

"Thank you for breaking your promise.
I never would have known who I truly am
and what I am capable of going through
without you shattering me.
I had to scramble to rebuild myself, my life.
I had to learn how to cope without you,
when you were the one person
I wanted to come to with all this pain
and anger inside me.
I lost you that day,
but I found myself.

I know you don't think about it.
For you it was a simple decision to leave.
You didn't have to worry about the fall out.
The devastation I lived in for months.
The dark nights I spent crying on my bedroom floor.
The meals I missed because
I was so depressed that nothing tasted good.
The voice in my head screaming that I wasn't enough for you.

I grew to know myself.
I started out thinking my entire life
would fall apart without you.
But each day I grew a little more,
able to recognize that I needed to live my life for me.
Losing you wouldn't dictate where my future led.

SAD BITCH POETRY

It would be a different future than I thought,
but I've had to make new plans before,
so I could do it again.

Feeling so empty,
so void of meaning was terrifying.
There were days I wished I didn't wake up.
I have new scars from trying to get over you.
But I did it.

Thank you for breaking your promise.
You told me you loved me when it wasn't true.
You broke my trust close to beyond repairable.
We could have had thousands of beautiful mornings,
hundreds of dreamy vacations,
countless touches that would feel like home.
But you destroyed that for us.
Because for you,
it wasn't something you could see.
It wasn't something you wanted.

I wasn't what you wanted.

I was so worried that I needed you,
that without you I would end.
The truth is, I found myself.
I learned the things I am not going to put up with.
I learned the things that are the most important to me.
I learned that I can and will continue on by my own side.

EMBER GRAY

I will hold my own hand.
I will wipe my own tears.
I will comfort myself.

I'm still hurt.
I'm still fixing my broken pieces.
I'm still moving on.
But I'm making progress.
I'm working on myself and what I want to do.

It may sound strange,
and you probably don't care either way.
But I forgive you.

I forgive your lies.
I forgive your hate.
I forgive the anguish you have caused.
I don't forgive you as a way of letting you off the hook.
No,
I forgive you
because I no longer want to carry this with me.
I no longer have the space within me
to re-open these wounds.
You no longer care, so why should I?
I'm done letting you dictate my life.
I forgive you and move forward."

I rested my pen on the paper,
slightly crinkled at the edges

SAD BITCH POETRY

where my tears had stained.
I stood as my knees creaked from sitting so long.
The sun had set about an hour ago,
when I first sat at my desk.
It had taken all this time
to sum up my courage
to even put the words to paper.
I knew I needed to release this,
all of the built up sorrow and anger
I no longer wanted to hold onto.
But finding the words felt impossible.
The hurt I had gone through before
felt just as fresh,
like I ripped open my wounds
and bled all over the blank white paper.
But now as I stood and looked
at the small letter scrawled across the notebook,
I felt something new.
Something I hadn't felt in a long time.

An airiness began to bloom from within my chest.
My shoulders released their tension
and my knuckles fell from their tight balls.
I tore the page from the notebook
and took a sip of the last of my now cold tea.
A deep breath and a few steps
led me to the windowsill.

I folded the letter delicately
a few times making it a small square.

EMBER GRAY

As I looked out the window,
the dusk sky beckoned a storm from the south.
Dark gray clouds rose high
as the trees swayed gently
against the violet backdrop.
I brought my attention to the candle lit on the ledge.
I held out the letter,
letting the flames lick at the black ink.
The paper glowed
as the embers danced
across the letter's surface.
Small ashes floated from the edge.

A small twinge of something pulled
at the corner of my mouth.
I let it stay.
A grin felt almost foreign on my face
but I embraced it.
I had grown so much in the past few months,
I was ready to feel content again.
As the paper burned at the end of my fingers,
tranquility draped me,
filling me with comfort.
The paper,
now gone,
carried my past troubles and burdens.
Now I was free.
I moved to the overstuffed armchair
in the nearby corner and pulled a blanket against me.
The soft patter of rain against the window

lulled me to rest as I dozed off,
finally serene in my thoughts.

59

I hope you find
what you're needing.

I hope you
love someone
as ferociously
as fiercely
as I love you.

I thought we walked
at an angle,
one day meeting
to walk the rest together.

I hope one day
our paths may
cross again.

I hope you don't forget me.
I hope you don't regret us.

I hope you know
I will always love you.

SAD BITCH POETRY

a note

I have struggled with severe depression and acute anxiety–with a newer diagnosis of Borderline Personality Disorder–nearly my entire life. I have been fortunate to find medications as well as a therapist and psychiatrist that both want to help me get better and live a life with more good days than bad. It's a long struggle with a lot of hard work.

While I hope you have been able to understand and feel my words, if you relate too strongly, please know you can always get help. The National Crisis Hotline is 988. You can speak to someone trained to help you. Lean on friends and family for support. Consider medication and therapy.

I have been incredibly blessed to be surrounded by loving, supportive, amazing people in my life. Thank you to my friends and family for always loving me as I am and being there to help me pick up the pieces of myself on the days that seem impossible to stay alive.

About the Author

Ember lives in Des Moines, IA with her two beautiful dogs, Zoey and Bonnie. When she's not writing she enjoys reading, crocheting, and watching lots of YouTube videos.

www.ingramcontent.com/pod-product-compliance
Lightning Source LLC
Chambersburg PA
CBHW052227150726
48002CB00003B/1317